THE LITTLE RACCOON
IN MY YARD

written and photographed
by Mia Coulton

Look!

Look!

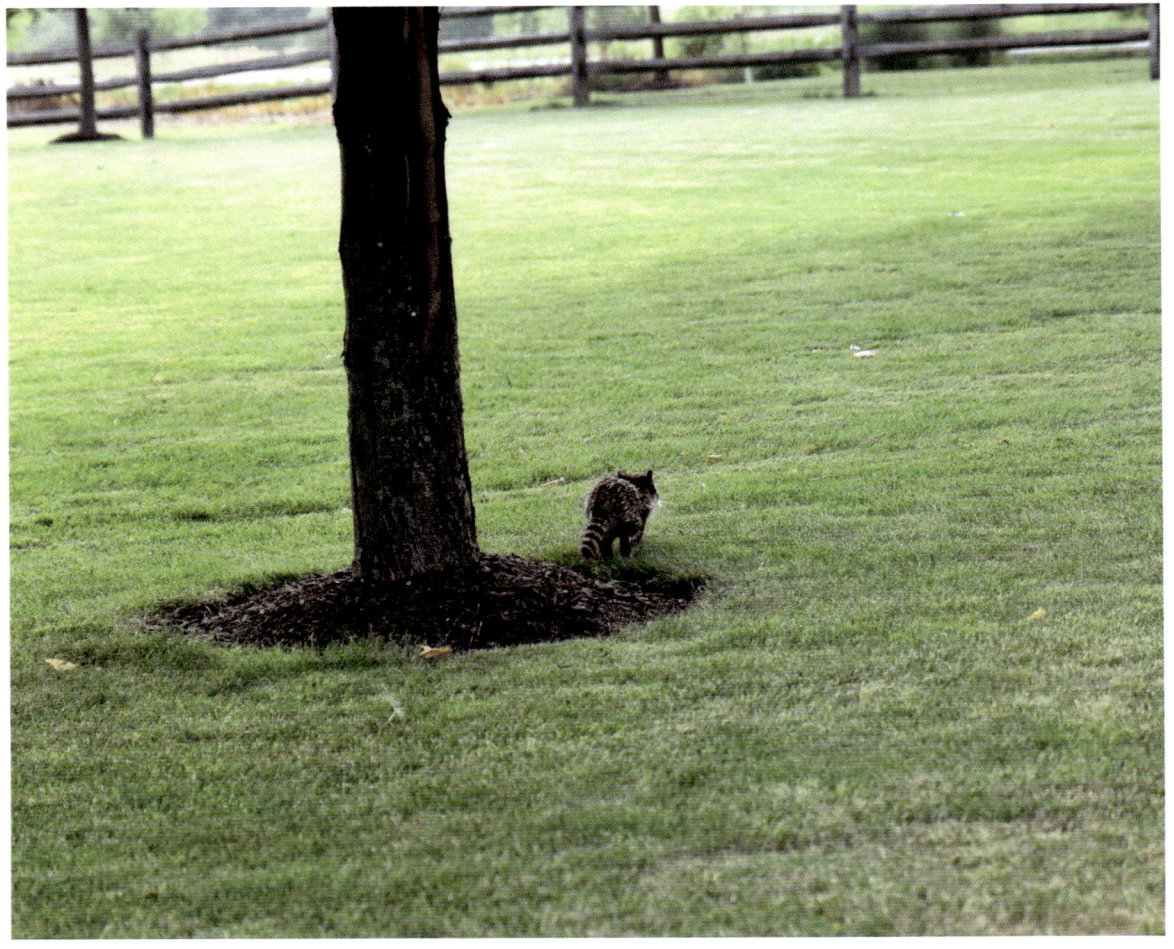

A little raccoon is in my yard.

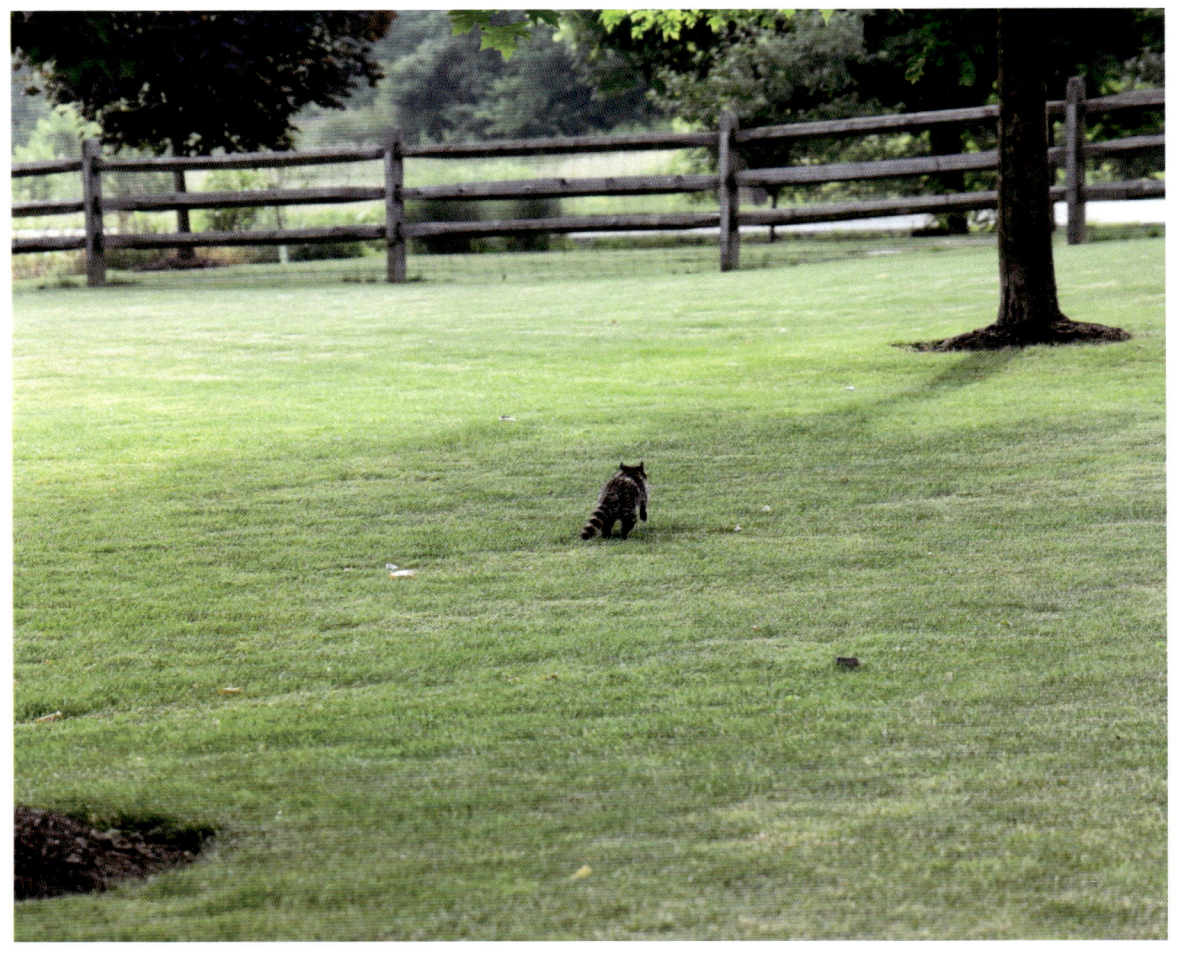

Look at it hide.

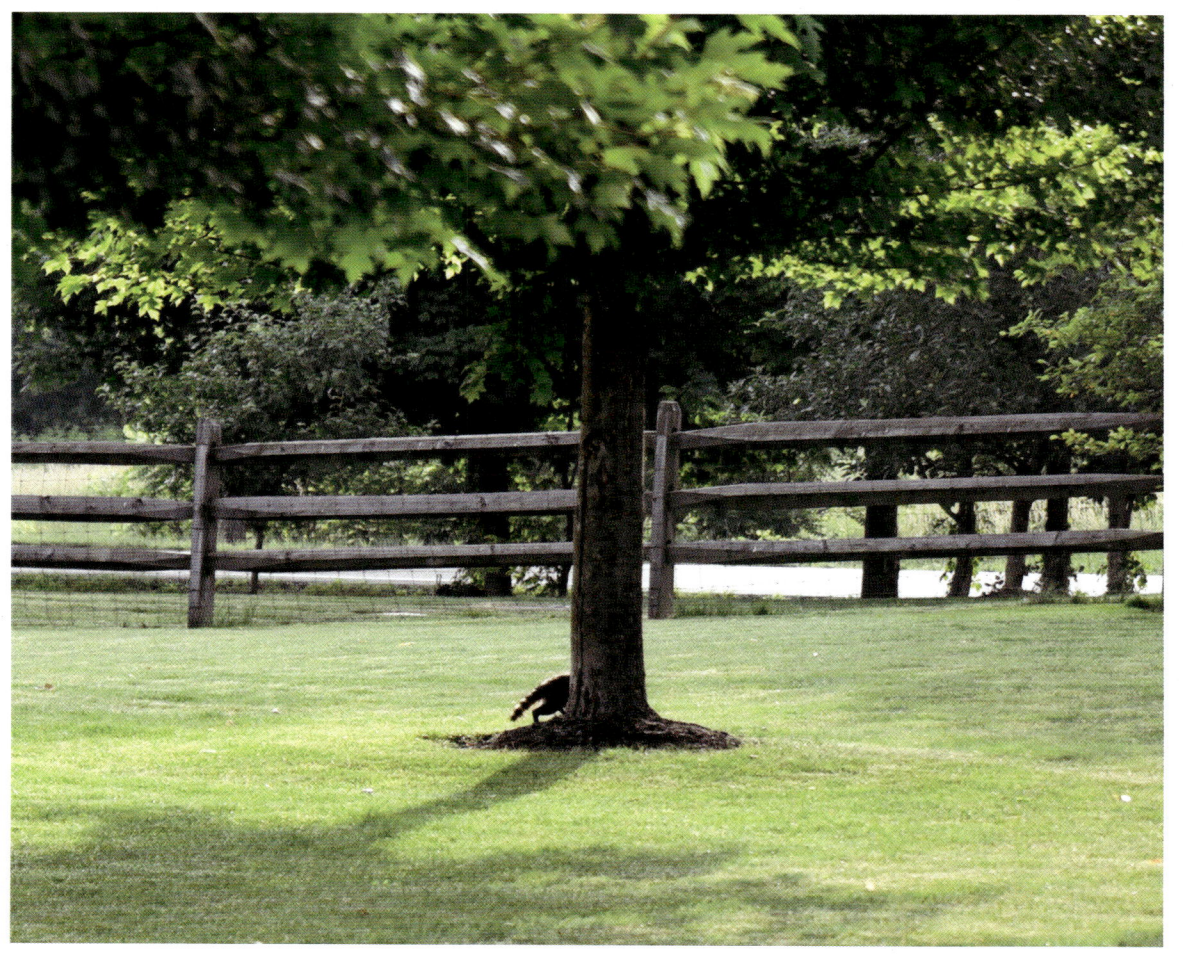

Look at it climb.

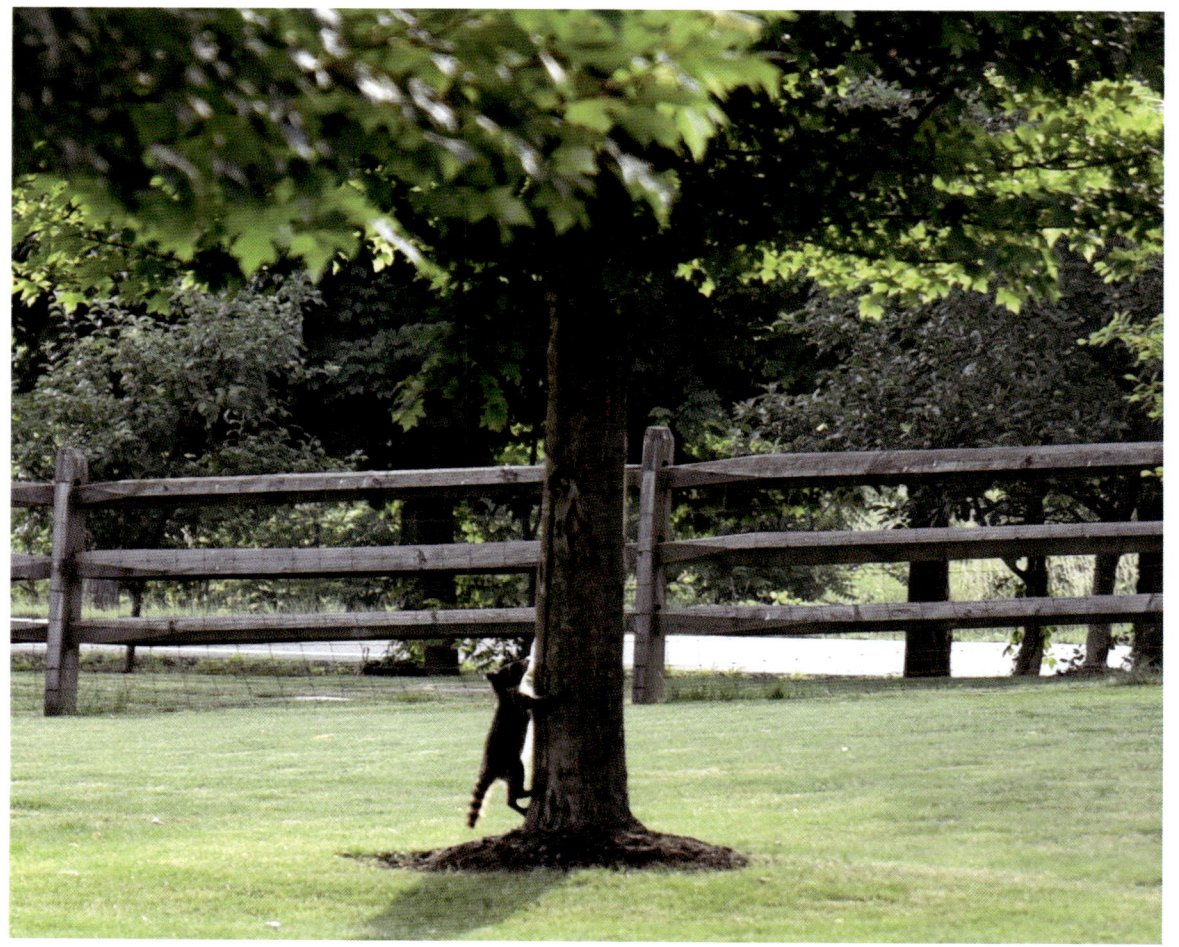

Look at it run.

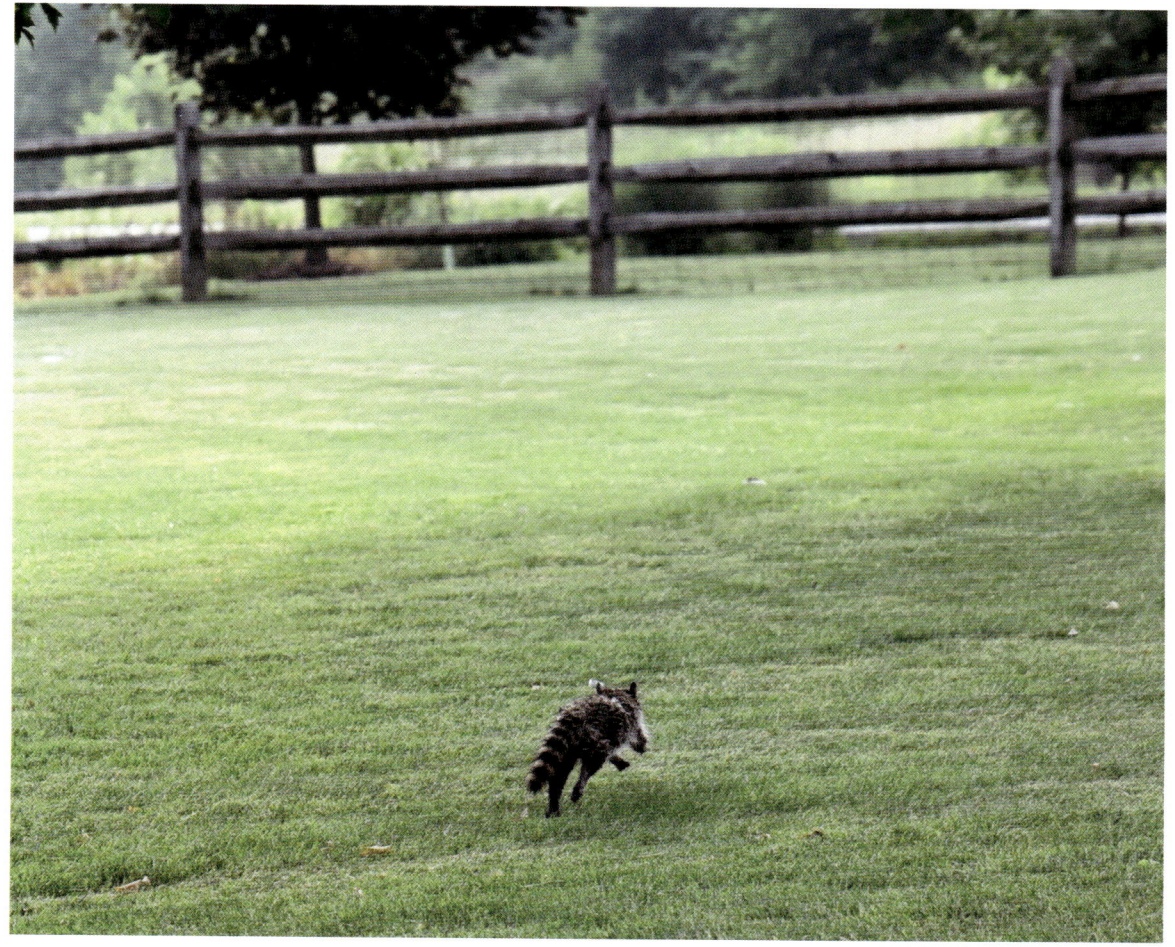

The little raccoon is in my trash!

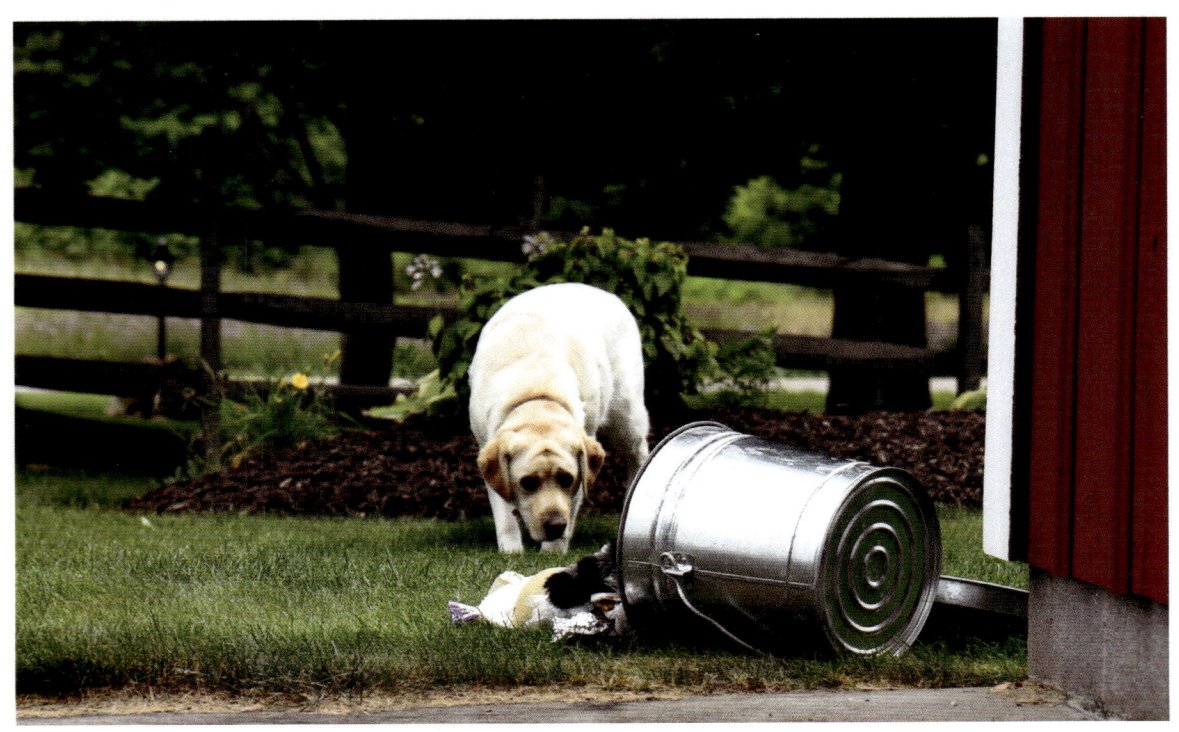